The Chick Corea Classics

Arrangements: Bill Dobbins

C Parts

ADVANCE MUSIC

Spain

Chick Corea

Friends

Chick Corea

Litha

The Loop

Chick Corea

Solos: 3 choruses, then D.S. al coda

rit. . . . .

Straight Up And Down

Chick Corea

A — Fast Jazz

B

C

Solos: play 6 times
(trade 8th's with drums last 2 times)

After solos, D.C. al fine
(play over the last chord)

E   Fm7   Em7/A   C#m7/F#   Fm7

La Fiesta

Chick Corea

The Chick Corea Classics

Arrangements: Bill Dobbins

E♭ **Parts**

ADVANCE MUSIC

Spain

Chick Corea

Latin (straight 8th's)

Friends

Chick Corea

Solos: 3 choruses,
then D.C. al coda

rit. . . . .

Litha

The Loop

Chick Corea

Solos: 3 choruses, then D.S. al coda

rit. . . . .

Straight Up And Down

Chick Corea

Solos: play 6 times
(trade 8th's with drums last 2 times)

After solos, D.C. al fine
(play over the last chord)

E Dm7   C#m7/D#   Bbm7/Eb   Dm7

La Fiesta

Chick Corea

Latin (straight 8th's)

Solos: 24x (6 choruses of 32 bars)

C#(7) D E D C#(7)

After solos, D.S. al coda (play all repeats)

Play 6x

F#maj7 Bmaj7/F# F#maj7 1. Bmaj7/F# 2. Bmaj7/F# F#add9

The Chick Corea Classics

Arrangements: Bill Dobbins

B♭ Parts

ADVANCE MUSIC

Spain

Chick Corea

Friends

Litha

Chick Corea

The Loop

Chick Corea

Solos: 3 choruses, then D.S. al coda

Straight Up And Down

Chick Corea

La Fiesta

The Chick Corea Classics

Arrangements: Bill Dobbins

C Bass Clef Parts

ADVANCE MUSIC

Spain

Chick Corea

Friends

Chick Corea

Solos: 3 choruses,
then D.C. al coda

rit. . . . .

Litha

Chick Corea

The Loop

Chick Corea

Jazz Waltz

Solos: 3 choruses, then D.S. al coda

rit. . . . .

Straight Up And Down

Chick Corea

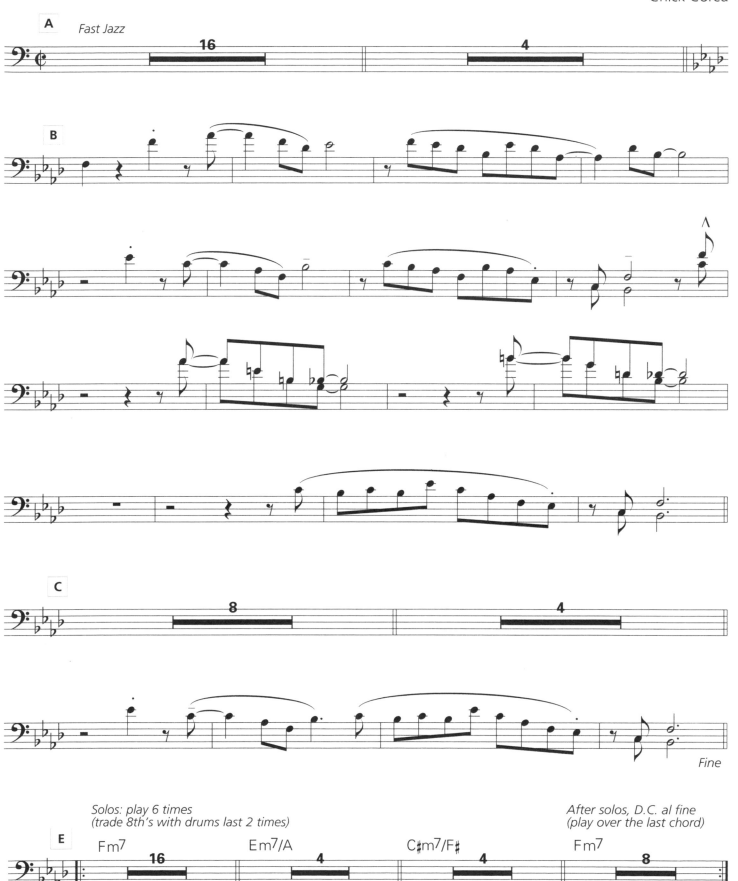

Solos: play 6 times
(trade 8th's with drums last 2 times)

After solos, D.C. al fine
(play over the last chord)

La Fiesta

The Chick Corea Classics

Arrangements: Bill Dobbins

Piano

ADVANCE MUSIC

Spain

Chick Corea

G6/9 A7sus

Solos: 11 choruses

Gmaj7#11 **E**

F#7♭9

Em7　　　　A7

Dmaj7　　　Gmaj7#11　　　C#7alt.

F#7♭9　　　Bm7　　　B7♭9

D.S. al D.C. al coda

Gmaj7

G6/9　　　D/A#　　　Bsus(m)

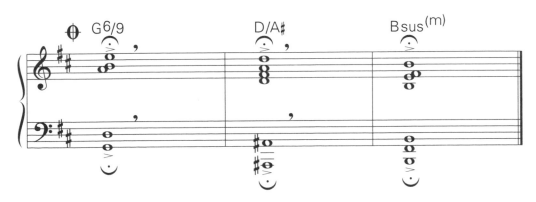

Friends

Chick Corea

Solos: 3 choruses,
then D.C. al coda

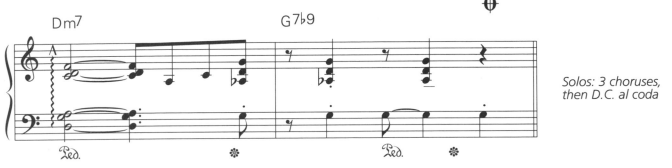

*Solos: 3 choruses,
then D.C. al coda*

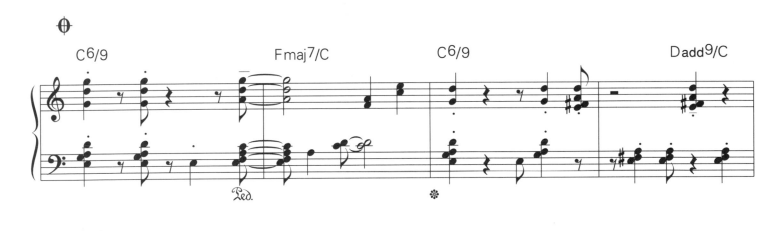

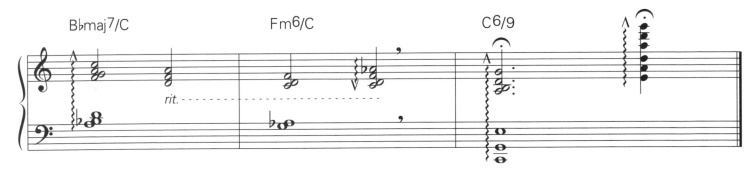

7

Litha

Chick Corea

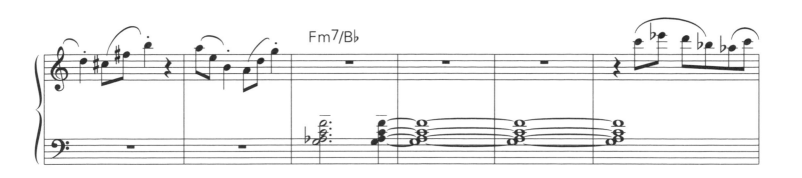

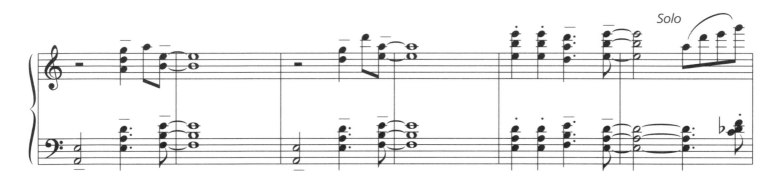

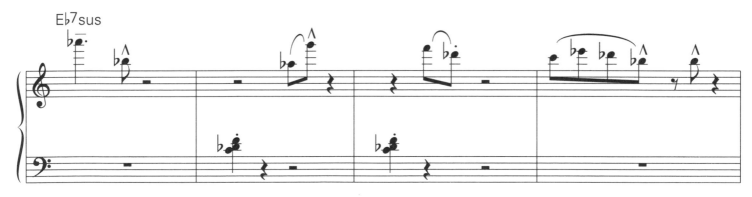

*Solos: 2 choruses,
then D.C. al fine
(fine 2nd time)*

The Loop

Chick Corea

Solos: 3 choruses, then
D.S. al coda

rit. . . . .

11

Straight Up And Down

Chick Corea

Solos: play 8 times (trade 8's with drums last 2 times)

after solos - D.C. al fine (play over the last chord)

13

La Fiesta

Chick Corea

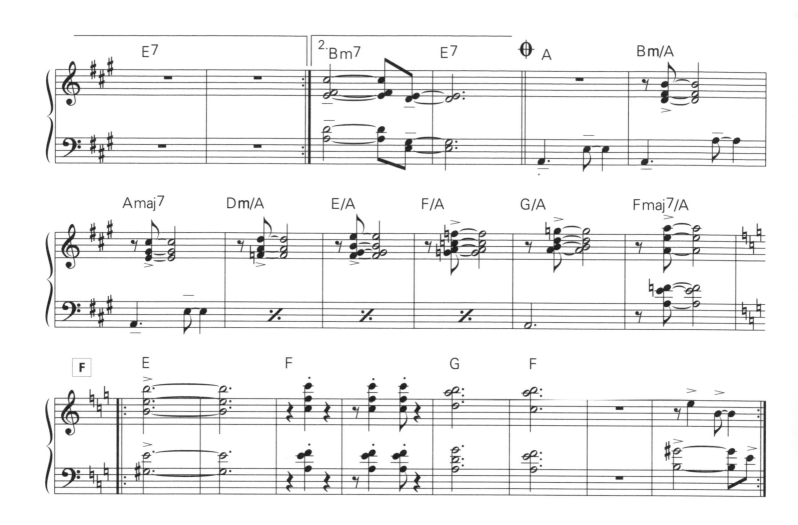

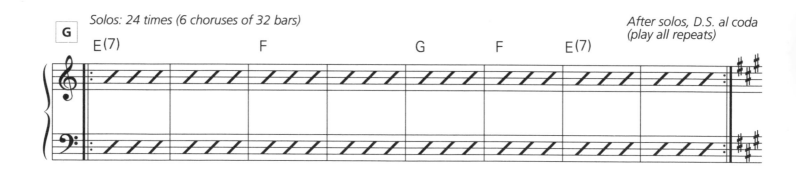

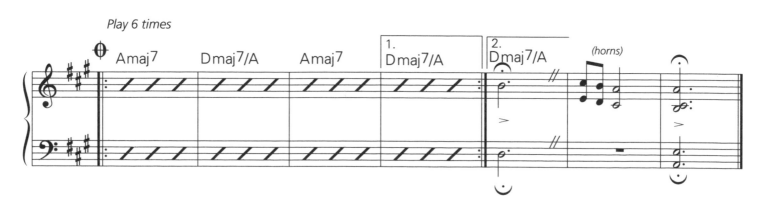

The Chick Corea Classics

Arrangements: Bill Dobbins

Bass

ADVANCE MUSIC

Spain

Chick Corea

Friends

Chick Corea

Solos: 3 choruses,
then D.C. al coda

rit. . . . .

Litha

Chick Corea

The Loop

Chick Corea

Solos: 3 choruses, then D.S. al coda

Straight Up And Down

Chick Corea

La Fiesta

Chick Corea